ELON MUSK
ENTREPRENEUR AND INNOVATOR

BY MARNE VENTURA

CONTENT CONSULTANT
Dr. M. Laura Beninati
Associate Professor, Mechanical Engineering
Bucknell University

Core Library

An Imprint of Abdo Publishing
abdopublishing.com

Cover image: Elon Musk discussing his car company, Tesla Motors.

abdopublishing.com

Published by Abdo Publishing, a division of ABDO, PO Box 398166, Minneapolis, Minnesota 55439. Copyright © 2018 by Abdo Consulting Group, Inc. International copyrights reserved in all countries. No part of this book may be reproduced in any form without written permission from the publisher. Core Library™ is a trademark and logo of Abdo Publishing.

Printed in the United States of America, North Mankato, Minnesota
022017
092017

Cover Photo: Ringo H. W. Chiu/AP Images
Interior Photos: Ringo H. W. Chiu/AP Images, 1; Refugio Ruiz/AP Images, 4–5; SpaceX, 7; Science Source, 8; Andrew Rybalko/Shutterstock Images, 9; Francesco Dazzi/Shutterstock Images, 12–13; Cyrus McCrimmon/Denver Post/Getty Images, 14; Shutterstock Images, 18–19, 33; Elena Elisseeva/Shutterstock Images, 21; Jae C. Hong/AP Images, 24–25; Paul Sakuma/AP Images, 27; Justin Sullivan/Getty Images News/Getty Images, 30–31, 45; Red Line Editorial, 34; NASA Photo/Alamy Stock Photo/Alamy, 37; Reed Saxon/AP Images, 39; Jens Wolf/picture-alliance/dpa/AP Images, 40

Editor: Alyssa Krekelberg
Imprint Designer: Maggie Villaume
Series Design Direction: Maggie Villaume

Publisher's Cataloging-in-Publication Data

Names: Ventura, Marne, author.
Title: Elon Musk : entrepreneur and innovator / by Marne Ventura.
Other titles: Entrepreneur and innovator
Description: Minneapolis, MN : Abdo Publishing, 2018. | Series: Newsmakers | Includes bibliographical references and index.
Identifiers: LCCN 2017930457 | ISBN 9781532111846 (lib. bdg.) | ISBN 9781680789690 (ebook)
Subjects: LCSH: Musk, Elon--Juvenile literature. | Tesla Motors--Juvenile literature. | SpaceX (Firm)--Juvenile literature. | Pay Pal (Firm)--Juvenile literature. | Businesspeople--United States--Biography--Juvenile literature. | Businesspeople--South Africa--Biography--Juvenile literature. | Clean energy industries--Juvenile literature. | Inventors--Biography--Juvenile literature.
Classification: DDC 338.7 [B]--dc23
LC record available at http://lccn.loc.gov/2017930457

CONTENTS

CHAPTER
ONE

BRINGING HUMANS TO MARS

E lon Musk stood on stage and looked out at the audience. Members of the International Astronautical Federation filled the room. Behind Musk was a huge image of Mars. The date was September 27, 2016. Scientists, space industry experts, and reporters had come to the meeting in Mexico. They were there to hear about Musk's plan. Musk is the head of Space Exploration Technologies, or SpaceX. One of his company's goals is to colonize Mars.

Musk explained his plan to bring humans to Mars on September 27, 2016.

THE FOURTH FALCON ROCKET

When Musk started SpaceX in 2002, he planned to buy a booster rocket from the Russian space program. This didn't work out, so Musk and his team used NASA technology to build their own. They named it the Falcon rocket. Their first three rocket launches failed. SpaceX was losing millions of dollars. Musk launched a fourth rocket in September 2008. It became the first privately built rocket to enter Earth orbit. During the same year, SpaceX got a multibillion-dollar contract with NASA to carry supplies to and from the International Space Station.

Musk explained his project to the crowd. He is working on building rockets that can take people to Mars. Musk believes having a second planet for human life is important. He thinks that in the future, Earth will experience an extinction event that will kill all humans.

MAKING A HOME ON MARS

Musk has a plan to make it less costly to send people into space. He is working to make rockets reusable. Musk has used technology from the National Aeronautics and Space Administration (NASA) to create

SpaceX launches a Falcon 9 rocket at Vandenberg Air Force Base in California.

rockets. NASA is the US space agency. It uses rockets that are not reusable. NASA has asked the government for money to build things such as reusable rockets but has been turned down.

Mars is the fourth closest planet to the sun. Earth is the third closest.

SpaceX is privately owned. It is not controlled by the government. SpaceX plans to build a 400-foot (122-m) tall rocket, passenger spaceships, and refueling tankers. Musk hopes to send people to Mars in the 2020s.

Musk believes Mars is the best planet to colonize. It's not too close to the sun and not too far from Earth.

LANDING A REUSABLE
ROCKET

The first stage of the SpaceX Falcon 9 rocket is designed to land safely on Earth after flying into space. It can then be refueled and reused. Before SpaceX, most rockets either fell into the ocean or continued into space. What is one advantage to Musk's plan for reusable rockets?

After liftoff, the second stage separates from the rocket.

The second stage boosts the cargo capsule into orbit toward the International Space Station.

The first stage slows down as it descends toward the ground.

The Falcon 9 rocket launches.

The first stage lands on a platform in the Atlantic Ocean.

A GREAT ADVENTURE

Musk knows colonizing Mars will be risky. However, he believes there are people who would like to make the trip. Musk compares colonizing Mars to backing up files on a computer. Like a backup hard drive, Mars could be a safe second home for people. He believes living on another planet will lead to new science discoveries. He thinks many people share his opinion that colonizing Mars would be a great adventure.

Mars has an atmosphere and resources that can be used to make air and rocket fuel. There is also ice on Mars. If Musk can figure out how to warm up the planet, Mars will have water. He also believes he can find a way to grow plants there.

Musk's challenging plan to colonize Mars is typical of his many projects. He has tackled big ideas and set big goals since childhood. He believes space travel and cars that run on renewable energy are possible. He wants to make Earth a better place. He works hard to turn his ideas into reality.

STRAIGHT TO THE
SOURCE

During his talk at the International Astronautical Federation in September 2016, Musk gave his reasons for picking Mars over other planets for colonization:

Just to give some comparison between the two planets [Earth and Mars]. . . . They're actually remarkably close in a lot of ways. And in fact we now believe that early Mars was a lot like Earth. [Mars is] a little cold, but we can warm it up. And it has a very helpful atmosphere which . . . means that we can grow plants on Mars just by compressing the atmosphere. It would be quite fun because you have gravity, which is about 37% that of Earth, so you'd be able to lift heavy things and bound around and have a lot of fun. And the day [24.5 hours] is remarkably close to that of Earth.

Source: Dave Mosher. "Here's Elon Musk's complete, sweeping vision on colonizing Mars to save humanity." *Business Insider*. Business Insider, September 29, 2016. Web. Accessed February 7, 2017.

Back It Up

Musk uses evidence to support a point. Write a paragraph describing the point he is making. Then write down two or three pieces of evidence he uses to make the point.

CHAPTER
TWO

GROWING UP IN SOUTH AFRICA

Elon was born on June 28, 1971, in Pretoria, South Africa. His father, Errol, was an engineer. His mother, Maye, was a model and dietitian. Elon also has a younger brother, Kimbal, and sister, Tosca.

Elon was an eager reader and quick learner. He was often quiet and withdrawn. In school he read all of the science, fantasy, and science fiction books at the library. When he couldn't convince the librarian to order more, he read the *Encyclopedia Britannica*. In middle and high school he hung out at the

Elon was born in Pretoria, South Africa.

mall bookstore. When the shopkeepers didn't chase him out, he would stay and read after school until dinnertime.

A PASSION FOR TECHNOLOGY

When he was nine, Elon's parents divorced. Elon and Kimbal lived with their father. Errol took them on business trips around the world.

In 1980, when Elon was almost ten years old, personal computers were brand new. Elon saw a personal computer at an electronics store. He convinced his father to buy it.

Elon's father, Errol Musk, encouraged his son's interest in computers.

The computer came with a booklet for learning a simple programming language. Elon was interested in the idea of creating a program that would make the machine follow his instructions. Elon worked through six months' worth of lessons in three days.

Elon continued to work on his programming skills. He convinced his father to take him to an adult computer class at a university. Afterward, he created a video game. He sold it to a magazine for $500. At the age of 12, he had started his career in business and technology.

SAVING THE WORLD

When he was a child, the superheroes in Elon's favorite science fiction novels and comic books inspired him to create a video game. It was called Blastar. The goal of Blastar was to destroy an alien spacecraft carrying bombs and imaginary weapons. Today, Musk hopes to help save the world by building a real spacecraft to colonize Mars.

A PLAN FOR THE FUTURE

There were plenty of books for Elon to read at his father's house.

He enjoyed using his computer and having fun with his brother and cousins. But school was a hard place for Elon. He had trouble making friends. Other kids bullied him. Once, he was beaten up so badly he spent a week in the hospital.

As he learned about the world from reading and traveling, Elon decided he wanted to live in North America. New inventions in technology were happening there. He couldn't talk his father into moving to the United States. So Elon decided he would go by himself.

EXPLORE ONLINE

Chapter Two talks about Musk's childhood and his interest in technology. Go to the website below and read more about Musk's background. Compare and contrast the information given in Chapter Two with the information on the website. What new information did you learn from the website?

ELON MUSK BIOGRAPHY
abdocorelibrary.com/elon-musk

LIFE IN NORTH AMERICA

One reason Musk wanted to leave South Africa and live in North America was his love of computers. In the 1980s, Silicon Valley in California was home to some of the world's top technology companies. It was an exciting place for new inventions. Musk wanted to live there.

Musk's mother was a Canadian citizen. Musk was able to get a passport to enter Canada. He bought a plane ticket and left home at age 17. He hoped to stay with a great-uncle in Canada. However, when he arrived in June 1988, he found out the uncle

In Vancouver, Canada, Musk found a job sawing logs.

had moved away. He spent his first night in Canada at a youth hostel.

Musk traveled in search of work. He found many odd jobs. He helped out on a vegetable farm in a tiny town called Waldeck and learned to saw logs in Vancouver. At another job, Musk cleaned a boiler room at a lumber mill. In time he found some of his Canadian relatives. After a few months, his brother, Kimbal, his sister, Tosca, and his mother joined him in Canada.

Elon Musk went to college at Queen's University.

QUEEN'S UNIVERSITY

In 1989 Musk attended Queen's University in Ontario, Canada. Musk enjoyed college. He was no longer teased or bullied. He made new friends who shared his love for learning and technology.

Musk used his technology skills to make money while he was in school. He built computer systems and sold them. He fixed broken computers and solved other computer problems.

Musk studied business, public speaking, and economics. He liked competing with other students for the best test scores. He studied, worked hard, and got good grades.

COLLEGE IN AMERICA

After two years at Queen's University, Musk was accepted into the University of Pennsylvania in the United States. This was a step closer to Musk's dream of moving to Silicon Valley. Graduates from the university had a good chance of being hired by technology companies. At the University of Pennsylvania, Musk earned degrees in both economics and physics.

In college, Musk spent a lot of time thinking about his future and the future of humanity. He wanted to do something that would have an impact on the world.

Three areas he decided to focus on were the Internet, space colonization, and renewable energy.

In 1995 Musk was accepted into graduate school at Stanford University in Palo Alto, California. Finally, Musk had made his way to Silicon Valley. His brother, Kimbal, moved west with him. Musk decided to leave Stanford after two days. He didn't want to spend more time in school. He was ready to start his own business.

MUSK AND RENEWABLE ENERGY

One of Musk's class assignments at the University of Pennsylvania was to create a business plan. Musk described a plan to build a solar power station. He researched how solar energy worked. He then suggested ways to improve solar power technology. In another assignment Musk wrote a paper on devices used to store energy. Today, Musk uses those devices in electric cars.

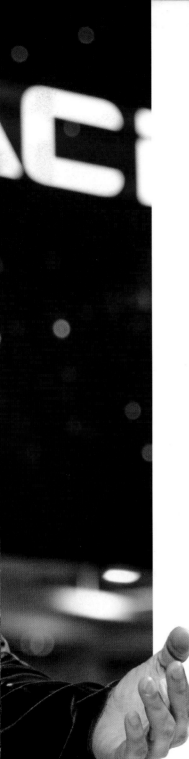

STARTUP SUCCESS

Musk and his brother, Kimbal, built their first company, Zip2, in 1995. At the time, the Internet was new to most people. People usually used thick phonebooks to find names, addresses, and phone numbers. Musk saw a way to change this.

Musk rented a tiny office. He wrote computer software that newspapers could use to make online lists of local businesses. People could go to the newspaper's website and find a restaurant or shop. They could

Musk started SpaceX in 2002.

even get a map online. Businesses paid the newspapers to be included on the website.

Musk and Kimbal worked hard to make Zip2 succeed. Kimbal visited newspapers to sell the software. The brothers hired engineers and salespeople. They didn't make much money at first. They slept in the office. They took showers at a local gym. Sometimes they could barely afford food.

Gradually Zip2 took off. The *New York Times* and *Chicago Tribune* paid to use Musk's software. In 1999 the Musk brothers sold Zip2 to Compaq for more than $300 million.

THE INTERNET AND THE WORLD WIDE WEB

In the 1960s, work by scientists and engineers led to the invention of the Internet. The Internet is a way to link computers in different places and share data. In 1989 Tim Berners-Lee invented the World Wide Web. This is a system of linked pages. As personal computers became popular, people used the Internet to access the World Wide Web.

PayPal was one of Musk's business projects. He ran the company with Peter Thiel, *left*, who was PayPal's chief executive officer.

MILLIONAIRE AND BILLIONAIRE

Musk had become a millionaire at the age of 28. He already had an idea for what to do next. He wanted to start an online banking company. Musk's plan was to create a better way to send and receive money online. He called his new company X.com.

PayPal was another online banking company. In 2000 Musk bought PayPal and joined it with X.com. Two years later, the online auction company eBay bought Musk's company for $1.5 billion. That same year, Musk married Justine Wilson, his college girlfriend.

Musk had spent the last five years creating Internet-based businesses. His hard work and new ideas made him a rich young man. Now he was ready to move on to a new adventure.

FROM THE INTERNET TO SPACE

Musk's new focus was on space travel. In 2002 he spent $100 million to start SpaceX. Musk's goal for SpaceX is to change space technology. He wants to give people the resources to live on other planets.

First, Musk put together a team of scientists and engineers. He and his team began designing and building reusable booster rockets and

DRAGON, FALCON, AND MERLIN

Musk named his spacecraft Dragon after the 1963 song "Puff, the Magic Dragon." He says he chose an absurd name because some people said his goals were not realistic. Falcon 1 and Falcon 9 are named in honor of the Millennium Falcon spacecraft in the Star Wars movies. The Falcon's engines are named Merlin in honor of a wizard in the King Arthur legend.

spacecraft. In 2003 Musk showed his first booster rocket to the public in Washington, DC. The rocket was named Falcon 1.

It wasn't until 2006 that Musk and his team were able to launch the rocket. Unfortunately, the Falcon 1 caught fire. The rocket crashed back to the launch pad. During this time, SpaceX wasn't the only project Musk was working on. He was also exploring ideas in the area of renewable energy.

FURTHER EVIDENCE

Chapter Four explains how Musk started his own space company, SpaceX. What are the main points about SpaceX in this chapter? Read the information at the website below. Does the information on the website support the information in the chapter? Does it present new or different evidence?

HOW ELON MUSK TAUGHT HIMSELF ROCKET SCIENCE
abdocorelibrary.com/elon-musk

MOVING FORWARD

Musk had moved forward on two of his three goals for making the world a better place. Now he was ready to make a difference in the area of renewable energy. In 2004 Musk invested in Tesla Motors. Tesla is an electric-car company. It was started by engineers Martin Eberhard and Marc Tarpenning. The goal of Tesla is to make cars that run on renewable energy. Renewable energy comes from a source that is not drained when used. Solar and wind power are renewable energy sources.

Most vehicles today use gasoline. Gasoline is made from fossil fuel. Fossil fuels come

Elon Musk introduced his third electric car, the Model X, in 2015.

MAKING A CAR FROM SCRATCH

Martin Eberhard and Marc Tarpenning created Tesla. They used a sports car built by Lotus, a British carmaker, as the starting point for their first electric car. They worked with Lotus engineers to create a car exterior that would interest traditional sports-car lovers. Then they designed the car to run on electricity.

from the earth in the form of oil, coal, and natural gas. Burning fossil fuels is harmful to the environment because it releases carbon dioxide. This leads to climate change. Gasoline is not a renewable energy source. In order to make more gasoline, more oil has to be drilled and collected from the earth.

Today at Tesla, Musk and his team make cars that run on electricity. Instead of a gas-burning engine, Tesla cars are powered by rechargeable batteries. Electric cars don't release carbon dioxide like gasoline-fueled cars. Electricity is clean energy. When electricity is created with solar power from the sun, it is renewable

The Tesla Roadster was released in 2008.

energy. Musk wants to create electric cars in order to fight climate change.

In 2006 Musk helped his cousins start a company called SolarCity. Its mission is to create systems that turn sunlight into electricity. Musk wanted Tesla and SolarCity to work together. In 2016 the two companies agreed to merge.

TESLA'S BUSINESS PLAN

Musk planned to create an affordable electric car in three steps. First he would build an expensive car. Next

TESLA MOTORS
CAR SALES

The graph below shows the number of all-electric
Tesla vehicles sold each year compared with the number
of gasoline-burning Toyota Avalons sold each year. Do
you see a pattern in the growth of Tesla's sales? How does it
compare with the gasoline-burning Avalon sales?

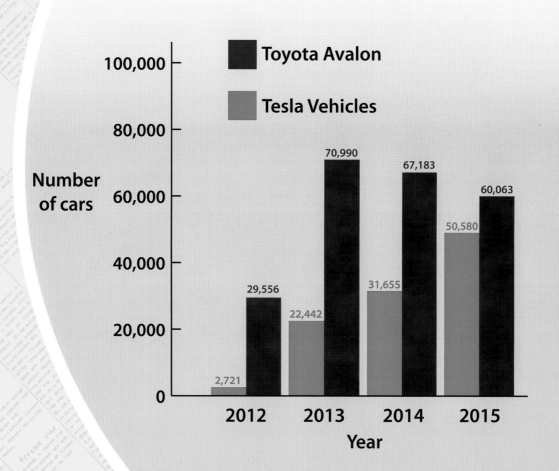

he would use money from those car sales to create a less expensive luxury car. Finally, he would be able to make affordable electric cars.

Musk wasn't sure his idea would work. He tried it anyway. Musk revealed his first sports car, the Tesla Roadster, in 2006. It had a huge rechargeable battery. It could go more than 200 miles (322 km) without recharging. It cost $100,000. Tesla sold 2,400 Roadsters. However, the cost of making the cars was more than the income from selling the cars. The company was losing money.

SETBACKS AND CHALLENGES

Musk had invested most of his fortune in Tesla, SpaceX, and SolarCity. Both Tesla and SpaceX were losing money. Other car companies were making electric cars to compete with Tesla. On top of that, Musk and his wife decided to divorce. It was a difficult time, but Musk didn't give up. He kept on working to make his companies succeed.

FIVE SONS

Musk and his ex-wife Justine are the parents of five sons; they have a set of twins and a set of triplets. Musk and Justine share custody of the boys. Musk spends most weekends with his children. They watch movies, make model rockets, and play video games. He hopes that humans will live on Mars during his sons' lifetime.

In September 2008, things began to look up. After three failed launches, SpaceX's Falcon 1 rocket entered Earth orbit. In December 2008, NASA paid SpaceX to deliver supplies to the International Space Station. Now Musk had the money he needed to continue his projects.

DRAGON AND FALCON 9

In 2010 SpaceX successfully launched its Dragon spacecraft on a Falcon 9 rocket. It was the first time a private company launched a spacecraft into orbit. It was also the first time a spacecraft was safely returned to Earth for reuse.

In addition to building rockets, Elon Musk created a spacecraft to carry humans.

Two years later, Dragon began taking supplies to the International Space Station. SpaceX also worked on a version of the Dragon spacecraft that could carry humans.

MODEL S AND MODEL 3

Tesla created its second car, the Model S, in 2012. That year Tesla sold 2,650 Model S cars. In 2014 more than 30,000 of these vehicles were sold worldwide. Sales continued to rise. The Model S was the best-selling electric car in the world in 2015.

In March 2016, it was announced that Tesla would be building a Model 3 car. One month later, 400,000 people had signed up to buy this car. The Model 3 was the third step in Musk's plan for the company. Musk planned to make a large number of Model 3s. This way, more people can drive all-electric cars. The cars were expected to cost between $35,000 and $42,000.

To make it easier for Tesla drivers to travel long distances, Musk began building Supercharger Stations across the United States. At these stations, electric car drivers can stop and recharge their car batteries

The Model S can go from 0 to 60 miles per hour (0–97 km/h) in approximately 2.5 seconds.

for free. As of September 2016, there were 705 stations worldwide.

A VISIONARY ENTREPRENEUR

Musk left South Africa at the age of 17 to pursue his dream of making the world a better place. He has made progress in his top three areas: the Internet, space travel, and renewable energy.

Tesla's cars can be charged at Supercharger Stations.

Musk used the money he made from his Internet-based businesses to start SpaceX. Today, SpaceX is sending spacecraft back and forth from Earth to the International Space Station. In addition, nearly 125,000 Tesla cars have been sold. This has reduced the number of gasoline-burning cars on the road and helps keep the environment clean. Musk continues to work in these three areas. Reporters, scientists, and space enthusiasts are watching to see what this visionary entrepreneur will do next.

STRAIGHT TO THE
SOURCE

In 2012 Musk talked about clean, renewable energy at the Motor Trend Car of the Year ceremony in New York City:

> *It is inevitable that we will exit the fossil fuel era because at a certain point, we'll simply run out of carbon to mine and burn. The question is really when do we exit the era, not if. The goal is to exit the era as quickly as possible. . . . That means we need to move from the old goal which was to move from chopping wood and killing whales to fossil fuels . . . the new goal is to move to a sustainable energy future. We want to use things like hydro, solar, wind, geothermal. We want to use energy sources that will be good for a billion years.*

Source: John Voelcker. "Elon Musk on Climate: Tax Carbon Appropriately, Tesla Founder Says." *Green Car Reports*. Green Car Reports, December 8, 2015. Web. Accessed February 7, 2017.

Consider Your Audience

Imagine you want to explain the information in this passage to a younger student. Rewrite the passage for the new audience so it can be understood by them. Which words would you change? What examples could you use to make the information more understandable?

IMPORTANT
DATES

1971
Elon Musk is born on June 28.

1988
After graduating from high school, Musk moves to Canada.

1992
Musk studies economics and physics at the University of Pennsylvania.

1995
Musk is accepted at Stanford University, but drops out to start Zip2.

1999
Musk sells Zip2 to Compaq and starts X.com.

2000
Musk purchases PayPal.

2002
Musk sells PayPal to eBay and starts SpaceX.

2004
Musk invests in Tesla Motors.

2006

Musk helps his cousins start SolarCity.

2008

Tesla releases the Roadster car.

2008

SpaceX's Falcon 1 is the first privately built rocket to enter Earth orbit.

2010

SpaceX is the first privately funded company to successfully launch, orbit, and recover a spacecraft.

2012

Tesla creates the Model S car.

2012

SpaceX is the first private company to send a spacecraft to the International Space Station.

2016

Musk explains his plan to colonize Mars at the International Astronautical Federation meeting.

STOP AND THINK

Take a Stand

Musk believes colonizing Mars is important for human survival. He acknowledges the high cost and danger of the mission but thinks there are people willing to take the risk. Do you agree that creating a settlement for human life on another planet is worth the cost and the risk? Or do you disagree with Musk about making life interplanetary? Write a paragraph stating your opinion. Support your argument with evidence from this book and the articles you have read.

You Are There

This book describes Musk's journey from South Africa to Silicon Valley and the startup of SpaceX, Tesla Motors, and SolarCity. Imagine you are a reporter and you have the chance to interview Musk. Write down the questions that you would like to ask him. Include at least two questions each about space travel, electric cars, and solar energy.

Surprise Me

Chapter One discusses Musk's plan to colonize Mars. After reading this book, what two or three facts about Musk's plan did you find most surprising? Write a few sentences about each fact. Why did you find each fact surprising?

Dig Deeper

After reading this book, what questions do you still have about all-electric cars? With an adult's help, find a few reliable sources that can help you answer your questions. Write a paragraph about what you learned.

GLOSSARY

colonize
to send a group of people to a place to establish control over it

dietitian
an expert on nutrition and diet

economics
the science of how goods and services are made, sold, and bought

engineer
a designer or builder of machines and technology

entrepreneur
a person who starts and runs a business

physics
the science of matter and energy and how they interact

technology
equipment that is developed using science and engineering

youth hostel
a place where people can stay cheaply for short periods of time while traveling

LEARN
MORE

Books

Conley, Kate. *Solar Energy*. Minneapolis, MN: Abdo Publishing, 2017.

Earl, C. F. *Private Space Exploration*. Vestal, NY: Village Earth Press, 2016.

Spetgang, Tilly. *The Kid's Solar Energy Book*. Watertown, MA: Imagine, 2011.

Websites

To learn more about Newsmakers, visit **abdobooklinks.com**. These links are routinely monitored and updated to provide the most current information available.

Visit **abdocorelibrary.com** for free additional tools for teachers and students.

INDEX

About the Author

Marne Ventura is the author of 46 books for kids. She loves writing about science, technology, new inventions, and the lives of creative people. A former elementary school teacher, Marne holds a master's degree in Education from the University of California. She and her husband live on the central coast of California.